CONTAINER G

WHY YOU DON'T NEED A YARD TO GROW VEGETABLES AND HERBS AT HOME, PLUS 17 BRILLIANT FREE GARDENING HACKS TO BECOME SELF SUFFICIENT EVEN WITH A SMALL PROPERTY OR BAD SOIL

Table of Contents

1

5

Introduction

Gardening at home is a great stress reliever and a healthy hobby. It also aids a great deal in the quality upkeep of your daily diet. Gardening likewise provides a fine recycling method for containers as well as assist in making sure you get ample clean air at home.

The great thing about gardening at home is that different types of containers can be used to create your garden. It could be a half barrel, milk jugs, or terra cotta pots. Any receptacle that can hold soil can be used if it has proper drainage in the form of holes at the bottom. If you are recycling a container, you can always bore the holes beforehand.

Technically speaking, container gardening is a form of organic gardening. In today's world where everything seems to be in a rush, growing your plants at home, in containers, can be such a cost, space, and time saver. Functional as the plants are, they also serve as great enhancements to the ambiance of any home.

The garden can be large if space allows for it or it can be nice, simple, and small. Almost anything can be planted in a container garden, from fruits to vegetables, to flowers to trees and shrubs.

The main thing to bear in mind when doing container gardening is that the container ought to be the right size for the plants being put in it. To be safe, it is best to get a container that is two sizes or one size larger than you require. This way, the plant will have the necessary room to grow and thrive.

The other element to having a great container garden is the type of soil that is used in the garden. Soil should not be taken from the yard and simply placed in the container as whatever pests or diseases are in the soil will simply be transferred to the container. It is advised that new soil be bought and used.

Container nursery can indeed convey instant satisfaction. There are rare things in our existence that can provide us the immediate gratification which a container orchard can. In a gap of a little time, you could go to a nearby nursery, choose a group of beautiful blossoming plants in fine fettle, fill a planter with them, as well as being rewarded with a remarkable, professional-looking garden. The added benefit is that you might never need to tidy it.

Gardening inside containers could suit whatever style you wish. You could go for a contemporary look, with bright lime grass inside an unambiguous white vessel, or a new formal array with matching vases filled by cascading floras flanking an entrance.

You could even own containers that will endure the wintertime, bringing happy green highlights to parts of your home which would then be insipid as well as boring. You could grow nearly anything within a container as almost all plants can be developed.

This book provides important knowledge in container gardening. Its main goal is to help you attain the highest level of benefits anyone can ever acquire from container gardening done well. It is my dire wish that you use the knowledge found in this book in your chosen endeavor.

Chapter 1: Container Gardening

What Is Container Gardening?

Container gardening can be a nice endeavor if you want to start a convenient garden. It can also be done no matter where you live. Having herbs in containers also means that their products can be within arm's reach whenever you'll be needing them. It also saves you a lot of space in your home, especially if you do not have a dedicated area for your container garden. The containers can also be aesthetically pleasing since there are containers that have great designs, so you are not limited to plain, boring, pots.

One of the concerns when dealing with container gardening is rain. Unlike in non-container gardens where the rainwater is distributed among the plants, rainwater can fill containers very quickly and drown the plants. Other than that, container gardening can be easy if you do the right things to properly take care of the plants and avoid the common mistakes made by other container gardeners. If done correctly, you will have an assortment of herbs readily available when need or want them.

People are naturally programmed to love plants and animals. Even if a person does not feel this connection to a great extent, they will always be happy to see vegetation around them, as it gives them a feeling of calm and joy.

With urban rainforests removing vegetation, many people have started to opt for pot gardening.

All potted gardening plants are grown exclusively in pots and are rarely transferred or planted in the ground.

Container gardening is still used in real gardens because honestly there is nothing prettier than a flowerpot overflowing with flowers, but it was more widely practiced for the opportunity it gave people to introduce some lush greenery into their urban abodes.

Is It Hard?

If you choose the right plant, pot gardening is easy, and anyone can get started easily. For beginners, pot gardening can be a fun way to grow plants.

However, pot gardening comes with its own set of challenges. If you're up for them, they won't be too difficult to tackle.

Of course, you must realize that pot gardening will not be a walk in the park. You're going to spend some time and attention on your small collection of plants to make sure your plants are healthy and growing well.

Does It Take Much Time?

Fortunately for you, container gardening is relatively low maintenance because you don't have to care for a complete garden. Gardens require daily weeding, pruning, watering, adding fertilizers, and other maintenance.

On the other hand, container gardening is considered relatively low maintenance. While you can't forget to water them or make sure they have enough light, you'll find them tolerably easier to maintain as they don't require much weeding or pruning.

Even with some more challenging plants, pot gardening is relatively easier to maintain and run if you can pay the slightest attention to the plants.

You only need a few minutes a day and a few hours a week.

Growing Your Vegetable and Herb Garden

Perhaps you are thinking that having a container garden would limit your selection to only ornamental flowers. However, if you've always wanted a vegetable or herb garden, then you're in luck.

Some of the enterprising and adventurous gardeners have discovered that it is possible to grow your vegetables, herbs and, if you feel up to the challenge, some fruit in a container garden.

For some people who didn't consider that possibility, growing their garden turns out to be extremely beneficial to their health, and sometimes may even be responsible for helping to cut down on their expenses.

However, many people like to say that if you are looking to grow vegetables and herbs, you should do so by choosing to grow an outdoor garden. On the other hand, there will be a group of people who are supporters of indoor gardening.

While your limited space options may push you toward one alternative or the other, to give you a fair shot at deciding, we will discuss the pros and cons of indoor and outdoor landscaping.

Benefits of Growing Plants in Containers

Many people consider gardening in a container for several reasons. It is a desirable method of planting compared to the traditional gardening system where tilling is required. Gardeners often complain of back pain, among other health issues, as a result of too much hard work done while gardening. Container gardening offers a concept that does reduce not only the chances of having these health issues but also gives room for you to explore your creativity while planting. Here are some of the several benefits you will enjoy while growing plants in a container:

The Luxury of Time and Convenience

One of the major attractions of this concept of gardening is the convenience that comes with it. It is such a secure system of farming that the elderly or those who cannot go out can adapt indoors. Unlike traditional gardening, gardening in a container gives you the luxury of time as the weather or general environmental condition does not limit them. You do not have to wait for a particular planting season before growing a specific plant. Container gardening makes it possible to grow plants anytime and anywhere if the right growing condition is met within the pot. This method of gardening makes gardening an acceptable practice for everyone and anyone, regardless of how occupied they are.

A Great Solution to the Issue of Limited Space

The availability or non-availability of space is never an issue when gardening in a container. This is because this method does not require a field or vast farmland before it can be practiced. You do not need a ground. You can have your plants growing perfectly on a windowsill, or a balcony, or anywhere suitable. The maximum utilization of space is one of the top benefits of container gardening.

The Growth of Weed Is Limited In Container Gardening

One of the disadvantages of traditional gardening is, having to put up with the weeds. This is very limited in the container if at all, it is experienced. It can also be quickly addressed without having to use toxic chemicals, which could affect the growing plants. Container gardening is, therefore, a suitable method not just for experienced gardeners but also for those with little or no experience.

Easier Pests and Diseases Control

The control of pests and disease is a major concern in gardening generally, especially in-ground traditional gardening. Failure to control pests and diseases will result in poor harvest or complete loss of the affected plants. The risk of this is, however, very minimal in container gardening as the effect of pests can easily be noticed and hence, controlled before it becomes a major problem. Pests and disease control in container gardening usually require little or no chemical application. This makes the harvest almost always chemical-free. In dealing with the pests, cotton buds soaked in rubbing alcohol can be used to eliminate pests like aphids, while brush can be used to remove larger insects.

You Can Grow Plants Indoor

The ability to move containers makes it easy to transfer the pots indoor. This could be either to protect them from adverse weather conditions or to give the home interior an appealing sight. Whatever the reason, plants growing in containers can do well indoors as much as they do outdoors. Everyone knows sunlight is essential to the growth of plants, but several plants require little sunlight, and they will thrive more quickly indoors. A provision could also be made for artificial light for plants that need more light exposure than they get from the reflection of the sun. For plants to thrive indoors, the right conditions must be put in place, such as keeping the containers near a window to enjoy the reflection of the sun or supplying artificial lights. This is a significant advantage for those who are mobility-challenged or too old to work under the sun as they can enjoy what they love doing within the comfort of their home.

The Benefit of No-Till Gardening

A container provides an easier way to grow plants without having to till the ground. Anyone who has ever had to till the ground knows how much hard work it is. In addition to tilling being a strenuous exercise, recent studies have shown that tilling the soil affects some natural organisms which are required for the growth of the plants. This makes the concept of container gardening appreciable as it provides the opportunity of creating a suitable growing condition such that the maximum result possible is obtained without digging the ground. Container gardening helps you to save time and energy because it is a no-till kind of gardening.

Less Need for Resources

The amount of water and nutrients needed to grow plants in containers successfully is less compared to traditional outdoor gardening. Growing plants in the ground require more water and nutrient because of a larger surface area which makes the water not only spread but also susceptible to evaporation. This is not the case in a container as evaporation is minimal and therefore makes the plants require less watering. This also goes for the nutrients needed by the plants. Containers require less fertilizer application, unlike outside gardening if the right size of a pot is used in growing the plants.

The Benefit of Moving the Container Around

Another advantage of this system of gardening is that it allows you to move the pot to a more suitable location. If you do not want to keep bending to the ground to attend to your plant, you can always adjust the height of your garden to suit you. If you need to move your containers to a better area from more exposure to sunlight, you can easily do so with a container. This is a benefit that cannot be enjoyed in traditional in-ground farming.

Easy Harvesting

Harvesting in container gardening is quite easy and makes the whole system more interesting. When root tubers like carrots, potatoes, and radishes are planted, they can be easily harvested by overturning the container on a plastic sheet. This is a more comfortable and accident-free way of collecting these crops, unlike digging them up where there is the possibility of causing damage to the crops in the process. With container gardening, harvesting has never been safer and more comfortable.

The Benefit of Choosing Your Growing Medium and Creating Your Growing Condition

In container gardening, you can try out different types of growing mediums to get the best yield possible. Some of the growing

18

mediums you could use include soil, expanded clay pellets, coco coir, peat moss, etc. This system of gardening allows you to create the best growing condition for your plants. You have the option of purchasing soilless potting mixes or create the growing condition for your plants. You can adjust the light, the soil pH, and nutrients to suit what the plants need for maximum yield.

The versatility, accessibility, mobility, and flexibility of growing plants in a container are some of the great reasons why it is the right choice for you. You do not have to worry about your garden whenever you change the environment and move to another location. Your container can also move with you to your new location. You can vary your garden's color scheme and give your outdoor the attractive display you want. Container gardening doesn't require many garden tools and equipment. You can always make do with what you have and start creating your garden according to your budget, no matter how little.

Methods of Container Gardening

Planning is everything when it comes to successful gardening – no matter what kind. A well-planned garden will, once planted, achieve exactly what the owner or developer of the garden requires. A badly planned garden will, in most cases, be unsuccessful in achieving this, and often this results in a loss of interest in the project and the

19

eventual abandonment of the garden. It doesn't matter what scale of container gardening you plan to adopt; planning is the very first step you should consider.

Gardening Goals

There are a host of reasons that you may choose to establish a container garden of any size. These goals will ultimately shape the size and needs of the garden. Establishing your goals should be your priority. Some examples are given below as a guideline but feel free to come up with your own!

Community or Social Goals: group gardening fosters the creation of social bonds and cooperation. For older people, it can provide much-needed company and activity, while for children it can create a safe environment in which to make new contacts. This applies to adults too! Group gardening can introduce a new level of cohesion within communities and at the same time produce healthy, fresh food for everybody to share.

Educational Goals: container gardening can be a great way to enhance learning about food production, the environment, and ecology in general. A container garden of this sort can be part of a wider community project or simply associated with an individual school. With many children being removed from experiences of real, live nature and food production it can be an invaluable way in which

20

to aid learning and interaction, which in turn promotes a better understanding of the need for sustainable agriculture and also for healthy eating.

Food Security Goals: this can be a community, food bank, or purely personal motivation. Not only do modern farming practices involve some unpleasant processes, but they also intrinsically hold the potential for food shortages. Food banks, meals-on-wheels programs, and other social enterprises may find the concept of the container garden a good way to source low-cost, highly nutritious ingredients. For individuals, the same is true, and the low-cost nature of this type of food production can be an important factor for many people.

Environmental Goals: whatever size of container garden you intend to establish, there will be some significant environmental gains. Air quality, even on a localized level, is improved as plants absorb carbon dioxide and produce oxygen. The increase in humidity in gardens, along with the rate of evaporation, also helps to create a lower ambient temperature in the immediate area. New plants and flowers will attract new birds and insect life, which is beneficial for biodiversity (this is the case, no matter how small your container garden and, although the global impact may be small, it still helps!). The impact of the use of rainwater or even wastewater from the home is also very beneficial in environmental terms. This reduces the pressure on the public wastewater sewers. Locally grown food using organic methods will, whatever the size of the garden, also reduces the use of chemicals and pesticides in use for food production. Again, this may only by the amount of one persons' use but less is more when it comes to pesticides!

Experimental Goals: perhaps you're keen to help save the world on a more professional basis; you can use container gardening techniques to test theories and practices and find ways to improve both the concept of container gardening and the production rates for food. Experimental goals may be ideal for schools, institutions, or community gardens, but contributing to our understanding of the benefits of container gardening and creating more productive techniques is also part of the fun for many container gardeners.

Personal Goals: for many people, container gardening offers an inexpensive way to relax, reap the benefits, literally, of growing their food and the practice can bring its rewards on this level alone. For individuals or families, many of the benefits listed above, along with creating a new, relaxing environment at home may be a priority.

Scale and Type of Garden

For those creating a small garden for their use, the scale and type of garden may well be obvious and limited by the available space. For those involved in community projects then these options may require more careful thought and planning.

For larger community (or similar) projects the following considerations may need to be considered.

Site characteristics and location includes the potential locations or the most suitable places to search for a location. The people who will use or manage the garden, the neighborhood, and any specific concerns relating to this and the environmental conditions, including climate, in the area.

Site descriptions for potential locations can include the type of location (rooftop, ground-level), the access to the site, nature of existing use, impact on (or from) neighboring buildings, immediate surroundings (including alleys or nearby main roads).

Implications for the local area can include implications for the neighborhood (both positive and negative). likely acceptance or otherwise in the area, suitability for long-term use, access to funding, and local regulations.

The Necessary Resources

For community projects and gardens defining the resources may be far more important. Planning at this stage can be crucial to the success of the project. List the resources you have, or expect to have, to hand readily. This includes people, financial and material resources. Next, it can be worth creating a diary or calendar to identify what resources will be required and when. Think about each phase of your project like setting up the garden itself, beginning the gardening, maintaining the garden, and closing the garden for the winter. For each stage of the process try to establish exactly what is needed in terms of people, finance, and equipment. In most cases, financial outlay will be important in the early stages, whilst "manpower" resources are more important in the latter stages. Clearly defining what is available and when allows you to discover any shortfalls in resources that need to be filled before you begin.

At this stage, you can list what you already have in terms of resources compared to what you anticipate you will require. This will be a good indication of how realistic the project is and whether you should cut back on some of your goals or if you are able to achieve more than originally planned. Where resources are lacking you may consider ways in which these can be found through fund-raising, recycling, or advertising for more volunteers.

Ultimately, your aim should be to create a project that is ready for launch but is realistic in its goals; this will be an almost certain way in which to ensure that the resources and requirements you have match up close and to create a foundation for a successful project.

24

This term applies to all flowering plants. Once the plants have finished flowering and all that is left are dead flower heads, the plants look very unsightly. Moreover, the dead flower heads also promote diseases to develop and also make the plant flowerless. Once the flowers start to decline, cut the flower stalk out; however, some plants do not require deadheading which includes petunias, vinca, begonia, and hibiscus as they often have the mechanism to de-head themselves once their flowers mature.

How to Get Started with Container Gardening

Container gardening is a developing trend that offers humans easy get right of entry to veggies, herbs, and some fruits. It allows anyone, even those with only a confined quantity of area, to grow, harvest, and use their very own plant life. Listed underneath are some guidelines to help you get commenced on field gardening.

Containers

The maximum important things you should keep in mind when deciding on packing containers are your budget, what type of vegetation you need to develop, and wherein you may develop them. If you're going to develop shallow root crops like onions, you will simply want small boxes which can be approximately 6-10 inches in size. If you want to add succulent vegetables which want more root area, you may have to spend money on 5-gallon boxes. Plastic boxes are the most inexpensive ones available. There also are boxes comprised of wood, however it is first-rate to keep away from them, as they are probably dealt with chemicals, which can also ultimately leak and get into your flora and subsequently into your food. Ceramic packing containers are excellent packing containers to use, although they may be additionally the most expensive. Whatever cloth you pick, though, simply ensure that they have suitable drainage.

Soil

Soil desires to be healthful, moist, and properly drained for vegetation to develop healthful. Make sure that the soil meets the requirements of the flora.

Space

The kind and range of flora you could grow will additionally depend upon how much area you've got. Before you go out and purchase your containers, make sure which you have notably studied the areas.

Chapter 2: Things Every Container Gardener Should Know

When it comes to container gardening, there are a lot of things you have to keep in mind that are very similar to when you garden in the ground. In this chapter, I'm going to tell you the things you must know to have a beautiful, bountiful container garden.

Drainage

Briefly mentioned in Chapter 1, drainage is one of the most important things to your container garden. It's a matter of life and death for plants. When there isn't enough drainage in a pot, the soil is going to become water-logged, and the roots of the plant will rot. This causes the plant to die. It's like having a bad heart.

27

The bad news is that most of the pots sold commercially do not have enough drainage. You can increase the drainage by drilling, carving, or punching larger holes into the container, but sometimes it's just easier to purchase a pot that has enough drainage. The minimum size for a drainage hole is around ½" in diameter for a small or medium-sized pot. For a larger container, look for a drainage hole that's an inch in diameter.

It is also a complete myth that adding pot shards, gravel, or stones to the bottom of the pot will increase the drain. Some believe that if you do this, you don't need drainage holes at all. Unless you're very attentive and you're able to water perfectly, you're going to need holes in the pot. Also, if it rains and the pots are exposed to the rain, then they're going to need holes.

Light

Most people wildly overestimate the amount of sun their container is going to get. While you can find good plants for almost any type of light, you have to know how much light the container is going to get before you choose a plant. To figure out how much light the container is going to get, set it where it's going to be placed and time when the light hits it, and when the light is no longer hitting it. You can also purchase a sun calculator to do this for you.

Without enough sunlight, some plants are going to shrivel and die. They'll slowly fade away into nothing and you won't know what's happening to them. With too much light, some plants are going to wilt and burn, so they're equally as unhealthy. So always be sure you have the proper amount of light!

Feeding

Most potting soil does not have any accessible nutrients for the plants, so you're going to need to add those. Most plants are going to need fertilizer added to the soil so that they can thrive. To begin, mix a slow-release fertilizer into the potting soil. Mix up a large batch in a bucket or fill the pot with soil and then mix in the fertilizer. You can use organic potting soil and organic fertilizer.

Next, fertilize every week or two weeks with a liquid fertilizer, like a fish emulsion or seaweed blend. It's going to smell disgusting, but it's going to help your plants grow and produce tasty fruit.

Many people will use Miracle-Gro, and once you start using that, you're going to have to continue to use it. Miracle-Gro and other synthetic fertilizers will kill the beneficial organisms in your soil, leaving it pretty much barren. Therefore, you can't switch over from organic to non-organic and back without there being consequences.

Make a List

You might not be fond of making lists, but you should do that before you go to a nursery. If you don't make a list, then you might be struck with plant panic. You become completely overwhelmed by the number of choices available to you so you either buy too much or you buy nothing because you can't seem to decide.

One of the best ways to avoid this is to decide what you want before you go to the nursery. This list doesn't have to be a list of exact plants, but you could go through an online catalog and decide exactly which ones you want before you go if you feel ambitious. The list can just have the number of pots you need, the size you need, where they're going to go, and the plants you can put into them.

If it's possible, it would be a good idea to bring the pot you are going to use or a picture of it with you. Most nurseries have someone there who can help you with your choices, and most plants are going to be labeled with how much sun they need and the drainage requirements.

Plant Good Neighbors

When you're considering plants that are going to be in the same container, be sure that they go well together. This means that all the plants in one pot or container should require the same amount of moisture and light. If you combine plants that have different needs, they're not going to thrive together. So, if you have a plant that requires full sun, such as a tomato plant, you should choose other vegetables that will also enjoy full suns, such as pepper plants or some herbs.

To find out what a plant requires, you can check the tag if you purchase it from a nursery, check the seed packet, or go online and find more information about it.

Save the Plant Tag

Plant tags are very important. They are going to tell you how big the plant is going to get, how much light it needs, what amount of water it needs, and the type of plant food it's going to need. The tag is also going to tell you if the plant is annual, perennial, and biannual. It'll also tell you the zones the plant is going to thrive in.

The tag is going to tell you about the habit, which means the plant's shape and how it's going to grow. It's imperative that when you consider the container design and how to arrange the plant, you don't put plants that are very bushy too close together. For example, if you have a large pot and you want to put some upright plants in it, you don't want to put mounding plants too close to them or they'll get shaded out. There are also trailing plants that might need support.

Try to purchase plants with tags if you're at a nursery so that you don't forget, and always keep the tag! It's also a good record for you to refer to the next year if you want to grow some of the same plants again.

Plants Will Die

It's a sad fact, but the more plants you grow, the more plants you're going to kill. Even the most expert container gardeners are going to kill plants, but the trick is to know when to give up on the plant and what you can do to save it. In a mixed container garden, it's harder to save plants because it could be detrimental to the plants that are surviving. So, you may want to keep larger plants that are picky, like tomatoes and peppers, in their pots.

When a plant starts to look bad, you can try a few different things. You can try to cut it back harshly and hope that it comes back. Just leave the tops intact and cut off any leaves that look bad. If you have a tomato that looks awful, you can cut it off at the stem, replant it in some soil, and keep it watered. It will grow roots readily again. That way you can remove it from the pot it's in if there are other plants. You can also remove the plant to another location until it looks better again.

You can also pull out the bad plant and put another one in its place. Depending on how dead the plant is, you can repot it and nurse it until it comes back, or you can recycle it in the compost pile. Just don't put it into the compost if it has blight! That will spread the disease.

Acclimate Plants

It's amazing how much abuse plants will take, and then suddenly they keel over for no obvious reason at all. Many plants do not like abrupt changes in their environment, so if you begin your container garden inside and plan to move the plant outside in the summer, then you want to acclimate them to their new environment over some time. They're going to need to be acclimated on many points: light, exposure to the elements like wind and rain, water, and temperature. This is important for young plants because plants that have spent most of their time in a greenhouse do not have the proper collagen built up in the stems to stay erect in even a light breeze, and they don't have enough melatonin in their leaves to keep them from burning. Treat them as you would treat yourself if you were trying to get more sunlight every day. Do fifteen minutes to half an hour at a time for the first few days, and slowly up the amount of time they spend outside over a few weeks.

This also goes for plants that have spent their time outside and are suddenly going to be brought inside to overwinter. If you decide to keep any of your vegetable plants over the wintertime, you must slowly bring them inside to acclimate them to the drier air and different air temperatures.

The More Soil the Better

There are many out there who will tell you that you should fill up your containers with all manner of junk like packing peanuts and pieces of a milk jug. While doing this will make the containers a lot lighter, it will also make them a lot harder to maintain because they will dry out quicker.

The more potting soil you have, the more water retention you're going to have. That will give you a much greater margin for error when it comes to watering and feeding plants.

Garden How You Live

The truth is this, container gardening is hard work. It takes time, attention, and money to do. There is no such thing as a foolproof gardening system or plant. Even if you do everything just right, some plants are going to thrive, and others are not.

This is good and bad news. All the uncertainty can make this entire journey very rewarding, exciting, and interesting. To have the most fun and increase your chances of success with gardens, assess how you like to live before you start this project.

If you don't like to water, there are container gardens that will work with your lifestyle. If you don't like to spend a lot of money, there are plants you can use in small pots to make it cheaper. If you want everything to look more pristine, then go ahead and purchase some nice-looking containers to grow your vegetables in.

The Best Part About Container Gardening Is the Versatility!

So, the best way to sum up this chapter is that you need drainage, proper lighting, proper fertilization, a good list, knowledge of what plants go together, the plant tag, the understanding that plants will die, knowledge about how to acclimate plants, the proper amount of soil, and a good understanding of how you like to garden. When you have all of that together, you can move on to the next chapter, things that can go wrong with container gardening, and how to avoid them.

Chapter 3: The Right Pots

Choose the Right Container

When it comes to container gardening, the type and size of the container will be very important. The more soil you can give your plants, the better off they will be. However, there are limitations to everything.

In general, the largest possible container will be best for your plants. Little ones tend to dry faster and need daily watering. Automatic watering pots that are for balconies and urban patios will extend the time between watering. You'll also want to think about the weight of the container once it's been filled with moist soil and plant material. It will be heavy! Also, there is an appearance. What will look good with your decor and your other plants? Cloth pots can even be used to grow vegetables!

The most important thing to think about is the depth of the container. Plants that have deep root systems will be stunted and unhealthy if they are not in the right amount of space. Remember, the deeper the pot, the greater the amount of moist soil there will be and the less often you will need to water. The exception to this rule is planters with automatic irrigation. In that case, the depth of the planting area may be minimal, as the moisture provided by the water reservoir below the planting area will keep it moist.

The layout of the containers to be chosen and used is a demonstration of the design objectives set by the gardener based on his/her bias and the availability of these materials.

With some talent, the native materials available in the locality can be transformed into gorgeously looking containers, like cut wooden poles or others. Only the imagination of the grower sets the boundaries. If the aim is to recycle and make long-term use of objects that are usually dumped into the trash, then use old tires, sacks, soda cans, plastic bottles, etc.

The most readily available containers involve medium-sized plastic, much used only to hold ice cream or any other food products, and five-gallon transparent plastic containers that can be acquired from restaurants, bakeries, or marketplaces (wash containers with soap and warm water before use). The total depth and width of the container will be determined by what you plan to plant.

Choosing the Right Pot For Each Plant

Get creative when picking up plant pots. You can use any potting material as long as it doesn't get too hot in the sun and drain well. If the pots you choose don't have enough drain holes, be sure to make some good-sized holes in them. If you can't drill holes in a particular pot, however, you can fix it by planting in a different pot and placing it in your preferred container.

You should also consider the size of the plants you would grow when choosing a pot. If you prefer a smaller container, the soil may not be able to get enough moisture, in a short time the plants will become attached to the root and dry out, leading to the destruction of the plant. On the other hand, if your container is vast, your crops could use all of their energy to developing roots and not enough to grow. The University of West Virginia Extension Service stated that shallow-rooted plants like herbs, peppers, lettuce, and most annuals require a pot no less than six inches in diameter with eight inches of soil depth. Larger containers, such as ½ barrels of whiskey and the bushel basket, are suitable for growing beans, cucumbers,

Flowerpots and planters are available in many different shapes, sizes, and materials. Regardless of the type of container you choose, consider the area where it would be used and plan accordingly— select containers in quantity appropriate to the size of the plant.

Several different types of containers are commercially available; although, you can turn almost anything into a container! Many are starting to use cloth bags to make their hanging gardens, and others are using milk jugs with the top cut off and some holes drilled in the bottom. So almost anything can be recycled and turned into a container garden.

Terracotta

Terracotta pots are affordable and attractive and have been used for hundreds of years. These traditional pots can be expensive when they are bigger and heavier, especially when they are full. If they are dropped or exposed to freezing temperatures, they will break. Clay will also dry faster than other materials, so it needs to be watered more often.

Terra Cotta is available in different sizes and shapes. The pots look great with their smooth color that highlights the beauty of almost any plant. Product of a porous soil rich in iron, it has a breathing capacity that maintains the calm of potting soils and drains excess moisture from the roots of the plants to maintain their state of health.

The major problems with terracotta are that it can dry quickly, particularly in hot weather, and is quite fragile (it can easily break). Some producers choose enameled terracotta pots as they get much better water.

Plastic

If you don't mind having plants that eventually grow to cover your pots or the look of the container, plastic is a better option. Plastic pots retain moisture well, are durable, and are reasonably cheap. They're also not heavy, making reorganizing your gardens an easy task. If your container garden is in an extremely sunny area, it is recommended not to use black or dark-colored plastic. As they heat up quickly and absorb heat, this can cause damage to the roots. The brightly colored container reflects heat and maintains freshness at the roots.

Wood

Wood is one of the most original and practical containers for gardening. They look good, do not shake, and retain water well. If you choose wooden containers, make sure they are made from decay-resistant wood, such as redwood or cedar, and confirm the quality of the build as the wood will naturally expand and shrink in the elements. Containers made of softwood or pine can also be used but should be painted with harmless paint to prevent rot. Wooden containers can easily be made with some scrap wood and some creative, stress-free idea.

Concrete

Concrete is ideal for supporting large plants that need more support to keep them healthy due to their weight. It has excellent insulating materials, protecting tender root systems by maintaining a calm soil atmosphere. With a concrete container, you can leave your plants outside in the winter without fear of damage (or even if you're planting in a public area) as it has the added advantage of preventing people from inadvertently working with your valuable pots or plants.

Of all the commercially available options, concrete pots are the heaviest and most durable. You will have to plan to place them in a permanent location and plan to spend a lot on the larger pots.

In general, you want to choose the correct size container. What it's made of will determine whether you need to empty the pot and store it in a basement or garage during the winter or if you can leave it outside. As a summary, be sure to check that there is good drainage in your pot and know how heavy it will be when it is full.

Enameled Ceramic

This type offers a range of colors to suit any garden style, and they are also durable. They are winter hardy but are expensive and heavy enough to move around. The plastic

Affordable, durable, and lightweight plastic packaging is a good choice for container gardening. You just have to shop around to find a style that suits your decor.

Moss Containers

Containers like this enable you to grow plants through the sides and through the top. They are mostly used in hanging baskets.

Metallic Containers

These types of containers absorb heat readily and are recommended to be used only for heat-tolerant plants.

Other containers used by gardeners are milk jugs, bushel baskets, planter boxes, etc. It is important to use containers that can conveniently accommodate the root of the plant you want to grow and give your garden the visual display you desire.

Container Size

Of course, the bigger the better, but there are some guidelines on what you can put in the smallest pots and what you might want to put in the largest pots.

Choosing a pot of the right size for your plants will ensure your container garden is a success. A pot that is too small is equivalent to a plant that will not produce as much, and you will have to work harder to keep them alive and growing. If the pot is too big, then you will spend more money on the soil than is necessary. Here is a guide to help you choose the right size pots for the right plant.

Of course, the larger the container, the higher the chance that your plants will grow healthy and strong. The advantage of using larger pots is that you need to water less frequently because the more soil there is, the longer the moisture will be held. However, if your space is limited, then you need to consider planting smaller plants that can survive in a limited space.

24" Diameter Pot

A twenty-four-inch pot will comfortably hold some of the following plants:

- Summer squash

- Large peppers

- Indeterminate tomatoes

- Artichokes

- Cucumbers

- A combination of vegetables and herbs.

18" Diameter Pot

Eighteen diameter pots will comfortably hold some of the following plants:

- Eggplant

- Cauliflower

- Broccoli

- Cabbage

- Greens and herbs

- Certain tomatoes

- Small peppers

The right container for tall tomato plants will be at least two feet wide. Indeterminate tomato plants will need pots that are at least twenty-four inches wide. Be sure to choose a cage that fits inside the pot.

14" Diameter Pot

The four-inch diameter pots will contain some of the following plants:

- Herbs

- Cabbages

- Cabbage

- Lettuce

- Spinach

- Arugula

10" Diameter Pot

A ten-inch diameter pot will contain the following:

- Strawberries

- Herbs

- Lettuce

You must remember that not all pots will be circular and tall. Shallow-rooted plants, such as lettuce, will be happy in a container of greater diameter than height. Use your judgment and give your plants plenty of room for the best harvest. Sometimes experience will give you the best advice for the future.

Container Preparation

Every container must have a sewage hole in the bottom so that the roots of the plant do not stand in the water. If there are no holes in the container, make at least four small nail holes on its sides ½ inch from the bottom.

All containers will require drainage holes to allow excess water to drain when the plants are watered. Roots allowed to stand in water are much more susceptible to infection and will sometimes rot and die. Tag three to five evenly spaced gaps at the bottom of the container and drill ¼ inch holes at these positions. The gaps will enable the surplus of water to drain. Often during watering, the potting medium will flow out of the drain holes.

Putting a piece of nylon window at the bottom of the pot can stop this from happening. Create a screen by putting the container at the top of the nylon window screen. Mark a location around the outside of the bottom of the container. Trim the ring out and put it inside the container before adding the potting medium. The container is almost ready to be filled with a soilless potting medium. This medium is light in weight and comprises peat moss, a bog plant with great moisture removal. This can be bought from horticulture centers in bags and bulk, and department stores in smaller quantities. This medium does not comprise nutrients, so you'll need to add moisture soluble fertilizers, such as fish emulsion, regularly.

The benefit of soilless mixtures is that they are pasteurized and will be less likely to cause infection. Ten quarters of the dry mixture will be filled with about three medium-sized containers. The soilless coco fiber may be dusty and unpleasant, and therefore, it is best to moisturize the content before extracting it from the bag. It will also require a reasonable quantity of water and a vigorous mix with a clean trowel.

When only a small quantity is required, shift the required amount to a container before moistening. The moistened mixture could then be transferred to the planting container. Fill the container before the level of the mixture is around one inch below the upper edge of the container. This extra room enables the water to be collected before the mixture is slowly absorbed. Rub the surface softly smooth to even out the potting mixture. Once you've collected your plants, pot, soil, and fertilizer, cover the base with plastic screening the drainage hole so that your soil stays in and the water can get out of it.

Don't put mulch at the lower part of your pot, no matter what you've read. It isn't going to help with drainage but is simply going to make drainage worse. Fill the potting soil container one inch or two from the top. Since your potting soil does not already have it, mix in fertilizer while carefully following the directions for quantity.

Organize the plants, bearing in mind the path your pot will be confronting. Dig a big hole for each plant, deep enough so that the top of the plant-soil in its nursery pot is one inch or two from the top of the container. You do not want to hide the crown (where the stem joins the roots) of your plant with the soil. As well, you need enough space to keep it from splashing out of the pot when you're watering.

Fill the potting soil around your plants, again, being careful not to cover the crown. You would like to ensure that there is soil around the roots of your plant and there are no air pockets. Water quietly and wisely, till the water goes out of the bottom of your pot.

Chapter 4: Tools And Accessories

Gardening can be done in several ways, but if you have chosen a container garden, you should have specific gardening tools for you to succeed. If you intend to acquire the most substantial part of your crops, you need to begin the planning before time. Purchase your seeds and garden equipment so that there will be time to sprout and germinate seeds.

Numerous gardening tools could be purchased, but the following are the essential tools for container gardening:

Small Shovel

A small shovel is perfect for pots. It makes it simple to dig in fertilizers and to plant your crops or seeds in the pot.

Hand Weeder

A hand weeder is a small fork class of tools with a long neck. It's useful for planting seeds and small plants and removing the little weeds that grow in containers. It can be used to dig a tiny hole to put the plant or seed.

Plant Containers

A plant container is a container for the crops, and it has to be the right size. You can make use of any container for growing plants and vegetable crops. Wooded boxes or crates, gallon-sized coffee cans, old washtubs, as well as five-gallon buckets can be used for growing vegetables in as much as there is sufficient drainage.

Small Cups or Egg Cartons To Start Seeds

You can use this for sprouting seeds. Ascertain your container is sufficiently broad to give room for the seeds to germinate. If you do not have enough space, the plants have to be transplanted as they grow. Also, you may need to buy a seed heating device as most times you a required to sprout them within, for it to be adequately warm so that they can germinate and grow.

Soil

Quality potting soil is a determinant for your plants to grow well. That is the secret to a successful container garden. If you use poor soil, your plants or seeds will not grow. The soil means a lot. Make sure you get top-quality soil that your plants require to thrive with or without fertilizer.

Plant Seeds

A plant seed can be flower or vegetable seeds. The ideal thing is to look for high-quality seeds if you are to plant vegetables to be able to harvest seeds and keep them for another season. Determinate tomatoes and shrub-type plants grow brilliantly well in containers. If you're looking forward to the best crops in your pots, go for these types of plants.

Garden Gloves

Though garden gloves may not be very essential if you are the type that easily got disgusted by dirt and didn't want stain beneath your nails, or sensitive to some plants, you need garden gloves. Also, if you do not want to lay your hand on a caterpillar, tomato hornworm, snail, and garden insects when removing them from your favorite crops, garden gloves do the job better. It will also guard your hands against thorns or all other sharp components of the plants.

Watering Can

Watering can do the job better by making the task of watering plants simple and trouble-free because water is running out of it in the form of trickling rain. You can, however, make use of a milk jug to convey water outside. But if you are to use it, ensure you gently pour the water in your hand and spread it with your fingers to enable the water to scatter and drop softly into the soil. If not, water coming from the jug may land heavily on the soil and splash on the crop's foliage, raising its danger of having fungus issues and other infections.

Trowel

A trowel is also an essential tool for container gardening. It is being used to loosen up compressed dirt as well as digging through trash in plant containers. Rather than using your hands, the trowel will get the task done better and faster and leave your hand dirt-free.

Pruners

A pruner is useful for cutting off dead foliage and pruning plants. Though you might think of using scissors, it is not advisable to use them. There are wet saps on plants which may leave remains stick and rust on your scissors. Cutting plants with scissors instead of a pruner also increases the risk of the plants being infected. Pruner is more active in cutting thicker crop stems, also enable clean cut while leaving your plants healthier in the containers.

Plant Organic Pesticide

If you are a non-fastidious type who could squish insects and not have a bad feeling, a pesticide may not be necessary for you. However, if the reverse is the case, it is ideal you have a plant-safe pesticide as part of your tools. Ensure you adhere to all instructions on its usage because it may not be right on food plants. Possibly, you can remove the pest from the plants and spray it on the floor with the pesticide.

Stick or String

These are essential for supporting container plants that needed to be upheld. An example is tomato plants (string and stick or tomato cage can be used to support tomatoes). They can also be used for young trees that needed to be upheld to grow in a straight line up and plants growing up the fence. Stick can be bought at your local garden store. String or yarn could be an organic color, like brown or dark green for it not to stand out in the garden environment.

Quality Fertilizer

Fertilizer is also essential for the growth of your plant. Having secured good soil, ensure you obtain a high-quality organic fertilizer to get the best result from crops. Compost can be in pellet or liquid form. You can buy specific fertilizer for each type of your plants like rose or citrus fertilizer. However, an all-purpose plant fertilizer does the job for most gardeners. Compost can as well be used to supplement your crop.

Potting Bench

A potting bench is also an essential tool for gardeners. Firstly, it serves as a platform to assemble and store your small appliances, plant marker, fertilizer, and the likes. You can also use it to conveniently move your planting tools from one place to another (for example, from your kitchen to your garden)

Each of the gardening tools is very important for your container garden to be successful. Make sure to have them at your disposal to ease work as well as getting the best results out of your products.

Chapter 5: Design Your Containers

The concept of container gardening is simple, but there is more to growing plants in a container than merely putting together a collection of plants. It takes a bit of creativity to have a garden that compels compliments from admirers. Your garden is not a garden until it is well organized and well arranged, such that it gives an attractive look and a refreshing feel. Below are design tips you can consider and work with to create a beautiful container garden of your choice.

Choice of Color

When designing your garden, the thing you consider is the color scheme you choose. You could try out a monochromatic color scheme, analogous colors, or complementary colors depending on the color of the container you chose.

Analogous Colors

Analogous colors are colors, usually a group of three colors that are close to one another on the color wheel. An example is a group of blue, blue-violet, and violet. Keep in mind that cool colors like blue are best fit for colored containers like terra cotta, and warm colors like yellow or red will go best with wood containers or, in some cases, terra cotta.

Complementary Colors

Complementary colors are simple colors that are contrary to each other on the color wheel. They are any two colors where one is the direct opposite of the other. Examples include a shade of blue and orange color scheme, red and green, yellow and purple, etc.

Monochromatic colors

The monochromatic color theme refers to different shades of a color. When you choose a monochromatic color, it gives an attractive look when a contrasting container is used to compliment it. An example of a monochromatic theme is a theme of purple shades – indigo, deep purple, lilac, and lavender.

Explore

You may as well creatively explore your choice of color for your garden. Go ahead and try out any combination of colors you want but ensure that it gives your garden an alluring effect.

Your Plants Arrangement

Plants arrangement is critical when you are designing your container garden. Usually, two ways of arranging plants within a container are according to their habit and according to their size.

According to habit: The terms used for plant habits are filler, thriller, and spiller. These three can be combined in a single container. While fillers refer to plants with mounding ability, thrillers refer to upright plants, and spillers refer to trailing plants.

According to size: Arrange your garden by grouping your plants according to their height. Arrange them in such a way that you have tall plants growing at the back and the small plants growing in front. Ensure that the groups of plant sizes you are putting together all complement one another.

Explore: You could as well explore and get creative with your plants. Try out plants with a variety of textures as spillers and fillers to make your garden design less stilted. You could also arrange your garden according to a similar pattern or function—for instance, herbs that grow well together, flowers complementing petal colors, etc. Don't be afraid of exploring your creativity. You never can tell how beautiful the result of your ideas will be.

Location

The last thing to consider in ensuring a perfect design for your container garden is the location of your garden. As earlier said, your garden is not a garden until it is well organized. You could turn anywhere and anyplace to your garden; the key is in the arrangement and organization.

Hanging Planters: If you are to use hanging planters, ensure that the background from where the baskets are hanging allows the plants' colors to radiate well. As a recommendation, using a white backdrop will help in achieving this alluring effect when the blooms from the several well-arranged hanging baskets start popping out.

Containers on the tabletop: You can utilize your outdoor furniture and place your containers on them. If they are well arranged and organized, they can give your backyard a brilliant attraction and a refreshing feel.

Depending on where you choose to create your garden, try to be creative with the arrangement. Utilize your doorsteps and stairs to create different levels of height and a general visual appeal for your garden.

How to Choose the Right Pot for Every Plant

In truth, there is no specific or right container to use for container gardening. There are so many containers that you can choose to use. You can decide to use pots, old jugs or cartons, or even watering cans. But to help you choose among hundreds of choices, here are some guidelines that you can follow.

<u>Style of The Container</u>

There are hundreds or even thousands of container styles. You can choose to use anything that you want at all. You can grow your plant in a clay pot, a fishbowl, in a shoebox, or even in a trash can. Your choice will be depending on your budget, your design preference, and the type of plant that you wish to grow.

Size of the container. Of course, the larger the box, the higher the chance that your plants will grow healthy and strong. The advantage of using larger pots is that you need to water less frequently because the more soil there is, the longer the moisture will be held. However, if your space is limited, then you need to consider planting smaller plants that can survive in a limited space.

Self-Watering Container

If you frequently travel or want a container garden but do not have that much time to tend to it, you can purchase a self-watering box to make sure that your plants get watered regularly. A self-watering container is very convenient to own. Still, if you live in an area where it mostly rains, you might have to monitor your plants more closely to make sure that they do not drown and die.

The ideal container for growing vegetables should be deep enough to allow your plants to develop a strong root system. Also, the container should have a minimum diameter of 24 inches.

You can either buy new containers, or you can use existing ones that are lying around your home. Terra-cotta containers are generally considered good choices, but you can also re-use your old plastic trash bins by creating drainage holes in the base to turn them into pots. To maximize space, you can also consider using hanging containers.

Attractive-looking containers are very inspiring and motivating, which is why you might like to consider using glazed ceramic planters. The great thing about them is that the material is porous, which will allow the roots of your plants to have access to air. If this sounds too fancy, you can substitute it with a polypropylene pot.

Each type of container has its pros and cons. For instance, clay or terra-cotta can break easily, especially by frost. Avoid using them if you live in the northern areas.

Cast concrete is very durable, except they are also very heavy and unsuitable for decks or balconies. Metal containers are durable as well, but they are heat conductors, which can damage your plants' roots. If you choose to use them, line them with plastic first.

Plastic and fiberglass containers are also sturdy and cheap, but make sure not to choose thin ones as these will become brittle and would eventually break.

Wooden containers look great and can protect the roots of your plants from fluctuating temperature changes. Pick only the rot-resistant variety such as locust, cedar, or pine treated with a non-toxic preservative.

Choosing a container should be easy. All you need is something that holds dirt and has holes in the bottom for excess water to drain out of. Easy enough, right?

The problem isn't finding the right container; it's picking from the plethora of proper containers available today. There are tens of thousands of containers out there, and most of them will do a decent job. You can go with ordinary containers and pots designed for container gardening, or you can get creative and use something that wasn't designed to grow vegetables in. The fact of the matter is you can grow vegetables in pretty much anything that holds dirt.

Here are some items people commonly use to grow vegetables in:

- Antique cans and containers.

- Boots.

- Buckets.

- Coffee cans.

- Colanders.

- Concrete pots.

- Custom-made containers.

- Designer containers.

- Enamelware.

- Fountains.

- Glassware.

- Hanging containers.

- Ice chests.

- Laundry baskets.

- Metal pots.

- Metal troughs.

- Old oil cans.

- Pans.

- Pedestals.

- Plastic containers.

- Pots.

- Terra cotta pots.

- Toolboxes.

- Trashcans.

- Urns.

- Vases.

- Wash tubs.

- Water coolers.

- Watering cans.

- Wheelbarrows.

- Window boxes.

- Wire baskets.

- Wood crates.

- Wood or metal boxes.

As you can see, pretty much anything that can hold dirt can be repurposed into a container for container gardening. This allows you to get creative and create containers that are interesting and unique. The material and type of container you use can reflect the style of the area where you're going to keep the container, or you can opt to go with something plain and functional. When you're using unconventional containers, it helps to stick to one theme. You want to create an exciting and unique look, not end up with your house looking like you couldn't control yourself at the local flea market.

Chapter 6: Managing Pests And Diseases

Regularly Inspect Your Containers

Containers such as wooden planters can become weak over time, thus inviting pests like sow bugs and ants to come to reside in them. As a result, they often damage your container more than the plant. When you see them present, remove them as soon as possible? Pests like these can do extensive damage, sometimes making it necessary to transplant your plants to a different container.

Regularly Inspect Your Plants

Be sure to check your vegetation for damage from insects. This will allow you to find what pests are causing the damage, remove them quickly, and prevent your plants from suffering major damage. You should be on the lookout for pests like snails and slugs. An easy trick for eliminating them is to simply place pieces of eggshells on the top of the soil. These pests find it extremely difficult to crawl over the rough surfaces and they will end up leaving.

Other pests such as aphids can be removed using strong sprays of water, followed by soapy water sprayed on bugs that are difficult to eliminate.

Get to Know The Pests Commonly Living In Your Area

While this will take some time to learn, this can prove to be time well spent. Some bugs are beneficial to you because they help get rid of the bad kind of pests. This means, if you don't know your bugs, you may end up eliminating the ones that you want to keep around. These good critters feed on bad insects such as aphids, as well as certain insects and pests.

Purchase New Soil Each Year or Sterilize The Soil You Plan To Reuse

Diseases such as fungi and some insects can reside in the soil and debris in and around your containers. If your budget allows, purchase new soil each year when the time to start your garden comes. If money is tight, you could consider sterilizing the soil you already own; however, while it is cheaper to reuse your soil, it can be an extensive process.

Make Sure the Plants You Have Chosen To Grow Are Native To Your Area

Some plants are more susceptible to pests and diseases than others, so it is especially important to avoid planting non-native types of plants in your containers. While some plants have managed to acquire their natural resistance, many will fall prey to pests and diseases if they are not normally grown in your climate.

Know Your Soil

Be sure to check the soil in your containers regularly. Not only is it important to know if the soil is moist or dry, but you also want to dig down a little into the soil to check for bugs burrowed in the soil.

Regular inspection will ward off the infestation, making the solution easier to obtain.

Make Sure Your Purchased Plants Are Pest-Free

When choosing plants, make sure that what you purchase is pest-free. If you accidentally purchase an infested plant, you may find it difficult or even impossible to get rid of the pests or diseases.

Maintain Cleanliness in Your Garden

Get rid of dead plants as they can be a breeding ground for different pests and diseases.

Eliminate Unhealthy Plants from Your Containers

One of the best ways to protect your plants from pesky insects is to apply fertilizers that can help keep your plants healthy and less susceptible to various infestations. When your plant is nutrient-deficient, it becomes weak and can attract pesky insects. If there are weak plants, remove them instantly because they may be infected and susceptible to attracting pests.

A Few Treatment Methods

Because you are growing foods that you and your family will eat, it is best to think about organic and safe methods in treating pests and diseases. Below are just a few suggestions you can try:

- Soft-Bodied Insects – Eliminate mealy bugs, mites, and aphids by spraying a mixture of Ivory soap, canola oil, and water. You can also use mineral oil, neem oil, or hot peppers to burn insects.

- Mites and Other Insects – You can make a spray bottle solution consisting of hot pepper sauce, Ivory soap, and water.

- Fungal Diseases – Create a mixture of baking soda and water. Spray the mixture on the affected plants until the fungal diseases disappear.

- Flying Insects – Use garlic or onions and liquefy them in vegetable oil tea.

- Snails and Slugs – Sprinkle crushed eggshells or lime in the soil area where the pests live.

- Fire Ants and Similar Pests – Use citrus acid and molasses or a mixture of garlic and boiling water.

- Japanese Beetles – Create a mixture out of water, liquid soap, canola oil, and molasses. Pour the mixture into a can and place a rotten fruit in it. This creates a great trap for unwanted beetles.

It is important to note that these sprays do not just kill harmful insects, but also the good ones. Make sure that you use them selectively, and only spray the affected areas. It is also wise to spray in the morning and after a rain shower.

If you are dealing with gnats, then it is wise to refrain from watering your crops for a while. Gnats cannot survive without water, and if you starve them, they will see your crop unfit for dwelling and disappear.

If the stems and leaves of your crops are infested with bugs, you can cut them off. Prune the infested areas and throw them away. Some plants can recover and sprout again regardless of how extreme your pruning is.

Using flypapers is one of the best remedies to combat whiteflies and aphids. You can buy flypaper and use them to get rid of the insects. You can also make flypaper by using a yellow board that's coated with adhesive. This will help eliminate a variety of pests that will be attracted to the board's color.

You can also get rid of pesky insects by handpicking. Although this method is slow, it is extremely safe. You can do manual handpicking or use a handheld vacuum to get rid of pests.

Common Mistakes You Should Know

- When dealing with large heavy containers, you wait for the end of the process before moving your pots.

Do not make the mistake of filling up a large container with soil and your new plants and then try to move it. Put it where you want it to be and then proceed with filling it with soil and plants.

- You drown your plants.

Make sure your container has plenty of holes in the bottom so when you water, the excess water can drain out. Knowing when to water can be as simple as sticking your finger into the soil to see if it is dry or moist. If it feels dry to your fingertips, then it is probably time to give your plant a drink.

- You deprive your plants of water.

While overwatering your plant is not good, under watering your plant is not any better. Many container gardens need watering at least once a day, especially during the summertime. For hanging

71

plants or plants placed in small containers, they will need watering more than once a day because they have less soil to hold water and moisture.

- You starve your plants.

Potting mix is the most common ingredient used in container gardens. Unfortunately, these types of mixes don't usually contain enough nutrients for the plants to grow and flourish for the season. To compensate for the few nutrients potting mixes have, you will need to feed them fertilizers. There are many fertilizers to choose from, but the right kind will depend upon your choice of plants.

- You are too cheap to buy good plants.

Like everyone, you may be tempted to purchase plants you see in big box stores at cheap prices because you think they will save you money. However, cheap doesn't always mean plants in good condition. Instead, try buying excellent quality plants from reputable stores because they are often healthier plants and have smaller chances of attracting diseases and pests. Reputable stores often offer a money-back guarantee if the plants prove to be diseased or die.

- You do not have realistic expectations.

If you are away from home a great deal, you need to consider a self-watering system or enlist the help of a neighbor or family member. Also, consider your living style and personality.

- You are afraid to prune your plants.

It is ironic that some plants do best when we cut off limbs. Tomato plants are like this. If you have too many branches, some of the plant's energy is expended on growing branches rather than producing fruit.

- You fill a large container with 100% potting soil.

If you are planning to grow shallow-rooted plants in a huge pot, try not to fill it with potting soil because it can be very expensive. Instead, fill in the bottom of the container with empty bottles, rocks, or anything that can take up space.

- You use the wrong-sized container.

Container gardening is not one of the many things that you can do mindlessly or without careful planning. Do not grow shorter plants in a huge pot as it can look stunted or plant vegetable varieties in a small pot. Make sure that you choose a container with a height and size that is proportionate to the number of plants that you want to grow as well as the size of the plant. If a crop will eventually grow tall, then choose an elongated container.

- You use containers with little to no drainage holes.

There are pots that are sold without holes or with a limited number of drainage holes. Refrain from using these pots because they can keep your soil too moist. This can result in rotting of the roots and death of the plant since there are no holes for excess water to drain out. Make sure you take the time to drill enough holes to let water drain out and to let the roots have room to breathe and grow.

- You recycle unsterilized containers.

You should not reuse your old containers without making sure they have been disinfected first. Wash the containers with soap and rinse with water or hydrogen peroxide. This will terminate bacterial growth and prevent them from infecting the plants you are planning to grow.

- You use disease-carrying gardening tools.

Failure to disinfect gardening tools can increase the chance of spreading pests and plant diseases. This is especially true if you have certain areas in your garden that are infested. Make sure that you thoroughly disinfect your forks, shovels, pruning shear blades, rake tongs, trowels, digging tools, and other gardening equipment before you use any of them on other plants.

• Chapter 7: 17 Container Gardening Hacks

Container gardening is less expensive than maintaining a regular garden; however, it can still cost you a lot. By merely planning how you would go about with your container gardening, you could cut the cost by half. How do you do this?

Assess why you are into container gardening. It is the foundation of your garden. If your motive is to earn, then you can plan the plants that you are going to have, the materials that you would need, and other pertinent data. However, if you have no solid reasons why you are into this, you will just do things without regard to the future, and you might spend unnecessarily. If you have finally decided why you are bent on having container gardening, then you can do smart planning.

Write down your plans. You would see the overall picture when you write down your thoughts, strategies, ideas, and blueprint of your garden. You would also be able to list down all the things you would need when you have a picture of your plans and not just a mental image. Plus, you could estimate the timeframe you need to complete your garden.

Make a to-buy list ahead of time and keep an eye on the costs. You can check how much you would need when you plan your garden needs. You could do your shopping at the end of the season sales and save money. Buy the items and supplies that you need throughout the year and store them until they are required. When you do not know the things, you need for the whole year, you tend to buy them according to the time you need them, and that could be costly for you.

Study how you would go about your plans. You can ask the opinions of other garden experts or enthusiasts or ask for help from friends or other people you know who are into container gardening. You could adjust your plans when you acquire better suggestions or ideas.

Thorough planning would save you money and cause you to spend less than necessary for your container gardening.

Start from Seeds.

Most seeds cost less than a dollar. If you would start from scratch, it may take some time and more effort, but you would save a lot. As you go looking for seeds for your container garden, you might find be confused with some of the terms used for describing seeds. For your clarification:

- F1 varieties or hybrids. These are expensive as the process of producing these seeds is more complicated than usual. The crossing of two-parent varieties is done so that a new one will be created.

- Genetically modified. These seeds are created in laboratories where their genes are manipulated.

- Open-pollinated varieties. Also known as heirloom varieties, these seeds can be reused year after year. They are found to be more resistant to various crop diseases.

- Organic seed. Grown without the use of pesticides, fungicides, herbicides, or fertilizers.

- For newbies, choose the "easy seeds" to plant. These are hardy and easy to plant, plus they grow earlier, too.

Buy Seedlings

Having healthy, young plants also costs less in the long run. They have a higher probability of surviving than seeds. Lesser efforts are required to ensure that they survive the transfer to another occasion. When buying seedlings, make sure to check the leaves; they should be green, and if there are patches of white or dried leaves, avoid these plants as they could mean weak or unhealthy plants. They may not last long when you transplant them. Check also if they are firmly attached to a group. Trying to separate and plant them could cause trauma to the plant and cause its death. Those planted singly are easier to transplant and have a higher probability of surviving a transplant. Also, do not just depend on the height of the plants to determine if they can survive. It has been noticed that smaller plants do better at staying alive when transplanted.

Buy All Your Garden Needs During Sales

It usually takes place at every end of the growing season. At this time, containers are marked down at half prices. Even other supplies such as tools and decorative supplies would cost less. Therefore, if you have any garden need that can wait until the clearance sales, acquire them during that time and save money.

Propagate Your Seedlings

Some seedlings are effortless to propagate. Instead of buying many of these plants, just be the one to multiply them and save money. Look for plants that can be spread only by simply cutting branches and putting them in water. When roots start to come from those branches, plant them in containers or pots. There is even something better than this. Some plants just propagate on-their-own. All you must do is to transplant them when they are strong enough to be transferred to a different container from the mother plant.

Recycle

Instead of buying containers, take a closer look at things in your house. Maybe there are old pails that you can use as pots. Old baskets can be redecorated and be used as vases in your container gardening. Be creative and imaginative and transform those old buckets or bottles into something useful. You would discover that there are many things in your house (specifically in your attic or basement) that can be recycled and converted into garden items.

Exchange Seeds or Seedlings with Others

Instead of looking and buying seeds and seedlings from garden centers, contact friends who are garden container enthusiasts and strike a deal with them. You can trade seeds and seedlings. You would not have to spend money at all, plus that is also building camaraderie with other gardeners.

Make Your Compost

Instead of buying fertilizers, you can make your compost in your backyard. Simply dig a small portion, and leftovers and other biodegradable things can be placed there. Not only have you saved money for fertilizer or compost, but you have also helped the environment by cutting the garbage being sent to landfills.

Compare and Contrast Prices

You can save money when you try to check different stores, flea markets, yard sales, and thrift stores. Sometimes, one tends to patronize a specific store, and he or she misses other great deals at different stores. You can also check online for the most significant sales and best offers of different shops. Look for coupons or vouchers too in your daily newspapers.

Choose Edible Plants

Instead of buying exotic and expensive plants, be practical and buy things that you could use in your kitchen. You do not only save money on caring for those strange plants, but you also save grocery money when you harvest your vegetables or herbs in your container garden. Think of all the herbs and vegetables that you always need in your kitchen like garlic, ginger, parsley, or celery, and plant them. Whenever you need any of these, you do not have to shell out cash. Just go to your garden and harvest from them. Plus, this might motivate you to start a little business and increase your income more. Neighbors or friends could just order some of your products instead of buying them in the local grocery stores. You could also try edible flowers. That way, you have house décor and ingredients for dishes at the same time.

Place an ad, use your social media accounts or the word-of-mouth advertisement and just inform other people that you are into container gardening.

You would be amazed at how sometimes people just offer many tips, items, or even plants for you, for free. For some people, instead of having tools or gardening supplies that are not being used in their homes or just adding spaces in their garage or sheds, they will instead give them to other garden enthusiasts if they know they require those. You save money, and at the same time, you have helped those people dispose of the items they consider as junk in their homes.

One does not need to spend so much. Be wise and use these tips and see how much you can save by doing so.

Sun Is Key

Most of the plants we nowadays use in cooking originate in the Mediterranean area and in places where the sun is plenty. Therefore, when you plant them, you should make sure that you place them somewhere where they can get at least 8 hours of sun every day. With this being said, it may be better for you to keep these herbs outside, but if you can only keep them on the inside, make sure that the place where you put them is extremely well-lit. However, keep in mind the fact that you should not leave these plants in full daylight for too long because this can lead them to shrink.

Make Sure That You Have Good Soil

Planters discuss "soil," however for containers, it's better to utilize something marked "potting blend," instead of anything named "potting soil." What is sold as "potting soil" is liable to be low quality and won't have the nutrients that your herbs need. "Potting blend" is lighter, made for the most part from natural matter, for example, peat or composted plant matter, and intended to give container plants the surface area and the drainage that they require. Work with your herbs on occasion, but not often, or when they look pale and less than great. Never utilize substance-based fertilizers because they can influence the taste of your herbs. Moreover, these sorts of fertilizers push speedy as opposed to moderate and sound development. Herbs that are developed excessively quickly frequently have fewer oils and flavors than those that developed more slowly. So, go simple when applying fertilizers. If you planted with a decent, supplement-filled potting blend, chances are you won't have to encourage your herbs regularly.

Compost Can Be Important

Since you will be regularly watering the plants, there is a high chance that the compost you initially mix with the dirt will be washed out gradually. This means that you may have to renew the compost composition of the pot.

Pay Attention to The Roots

The root is very important for the plant, so make sure you don't use compost that was mixed precisely to make the flowers grow. Also, do not collect the plants when they are blossoming, and make sure that you don't uproot the plant when you collect the herb you need. Rather than do that, use scissors to cut as much as you need out of it, leaving the root there.

Have Everything You'll Need

This may not sound like a bright idea, but most beginners will find themselves at a loss of things when they begin planting. They'd have to run to the gardening supplier and the stores to buy one thing or another very often, and this can get very frustrating at times. You may feel that you have all that you'd need, but when you are working, you'll realize that some specific tools can make work easier, or they would be better to use in certain circumstances.

Give Preference to Immunity

Science and technology have made tremendous progress. Pests and diseases that were unavoidable in the past are highly preventable. You can use a variety of measures, including pesticides and chemicals. However, you can also prevent diseases even without the use of chemical means. These days you can get several hybrid varieties of your favorite plants that are resistant to most pests and diseases. They have been engineered in a way that they don't attract certain pests and have stronger immunity against several common diseases. This doesn't mean that your plants cannot get affected by diseases and pests. It simply means that they will have a better protection mechanism against common enemies, and you can enhance the protection by taking some positive steps to avoid area-specific issues. It helps in decreasing the risk of a gardener considerably.

Work Hard During the Winter

Most gardeners think that because the winters don't have active plants, they can afford to get lazy in the winters. This is a myth, and the faster you get over it, the better it would be for you. The winters are work time as most of the constructive work related to preparation gets done in this period. You must prepare your container gardening properly. Weed out anything that's not needed. It would be better if you can simply mix some compost and give it a light shuffle. Do not overturn too deep; just mix some compost and level the bed. Early winters are good for pruning the trees and shrubs as the buds don't start forming yet, and hence the risk of chopping off a bud is low. However, if you think that this is a task you can even do, later, you are losing your precious time.

Mulch Every Time You Plant

This is a piece of advice most gardeners ignore without giving much thought. Some people think that mulching may make their container gardening surface look unattractive. You must understand that not mulching makes it even more attractive for pests and weeds. Another advantage of mulching is the conservation of moisture in the soil. This cover would help the soil retain much-needed moisture, and your plants would thank you for that.

Pay Good Attention to The Irrigation System

This is something that must be clear to every gardener. You will have to plan your irrigation system before planning your raised bed. If you are planning an automated irrigation system, then it will be placed inside the bed before filling in the growing medium, and hence planning is a must.

Chapter 8: When Winter Comes

Preparing the garden to bed for the winter is, for the most part, a matter of tidying up and concealing. As fall advances and temperatures drop, those plants that haven't yet been murdered by ice get ready for lethargy. Cut out the darkened stems and foliage of yearly blossoms and vegetables to prevent the likelihood of their harboring malady pathogens and bug eggs over the winter. The cool climate is a decent time to make an icy casing, dive, and box in raised beds and make general repairs.

While it shows up as though all action in the garden has ceased, there's a ton going on under the soil until it turns solid. Recently transplanted trees and bushes, divisions of perennials, and solid knobs are all developing roots, drawing on soil supplements and dampness around them. Worms and different microorganisms in the dirt are also preparing the natural material they're finding. Doubtlessly, the natural mulch you spread to secure the dirt amid the mid-year months has generously disintegrated.

Gardening calendar:

- This is the time of year to stop cultivating.

- Cut fall-shading hydrangeas for courses of action.

- Keep on watering enough until ice.

- Leave blossoms on hydrangeas for winter interest.

- Bring compartments inside after the main ice.

- Spread the base of the hydrangea with wood chips, leaves, and so forth for winter insurance.

The following plants can be planted during the fall:

- Asparagus

- Broad beans

- Kohlrabi

- Lettuce

- Onions

- Rhubarb

- Strawberries

- Berries

- Currants

Tips and Techniques

The short dull days and severe climate can make the possibility of planting in winter both ugly and conceivably useless. In any case, a smidgen of winter arranging can get the garden prepared for an awesome year ahead.

Clean

Accumulate all the instruments that you have utilized in recent months and give them a decent cleaning to evacuate all the earth and rust. Utilize a gentle cleanser to sterilize pots and seed plates.

Check Walls and Alike

Look at the wall, sheds, entryways, and different structures for indications of shortcoming or spoil and get them repaired before the snow and high winds arrive.

Garden Care

The garden needs somewhat of a breather over the winter months so keeping the grass out is the best thing to do. Make an exception to dispose of the huge weeds, greenery and clears them out.

Storehouses

Give sheds and nurseries a decent scour and sort out each one of those instruments you cleaned before. Spruce up tables and seats also.

The Vegetable Garden

Spread root vegetables, for example, carrots and parsnips with fifteen centimeters of straw and leaves, and they can be reaped all through the winter. On the off chance that snow is conjecture spread with an old bit of floor covering.

Manure

If you don't as of now have a fertilizer stack or receptacle, this is as great a period as any to begin one, with all the leaves and cuttings to be discarded. For the individuals who as of now have a container, a great blend will help the treating the soil procedure along.

Lists

There are few better approaches to spend a chilly winter's night than poring over a portion of the numerous mail request seed inventories longing for the developing season to come and arranging your optimal greenery enclosure.

Cover the Plants

Ensuring plants shed and the nearby untamed life is vital; however, bear in mind the solid plant specialist! Dressing fittingly and ensuring yourself against the rigors of winter ought to be one of your first contemplations. Look at the extensive variety of open-air attire at Blacks.

Moreover, whatever one does with the bulbs at the start of fall depends upon the toughness zone and the matching profundity of the ice line in one's district. For colder environments, you'll have to jump up and store handles in a cool, faint range until the danger of ice has passed. In case it's ensured to desert them in the ground through the winter, essentially ahead and reveal, confine, and replant any present handles that need upkeep. You can likewise plant new globules once the climate chills off. Ensure they have remarkable conditions and enough time to set up roots before the temperature drops too low. Wire bone dinner or low-nitrogen manure into the soil at the base of planting openings to commence root advancement.

Tips on How to Look After Your Garden In Winter

Looking after the garden in the cold season of winter requires taking extra good care of it in a more precise manner. In winters there won't be much weed to face, but yes there would be some other problems like lack of sunlight and excessive dryness in the environment.

In such a situation the greenery of the garden won't remain the way it used to during the other sunlit seasons of the year. Garden cares are the professionals which help in restoring the beauty of the garden s in the deadly season of winters as well. They provide extra care to the client's garden whenever required.

There are a few tips that gardeners follow to get the best out of their work. Such tips are:

- Using the time factor as little as possible.

- Mowing the grass only during a warmer day.

- Using a leaf blower to get rid of leaves that spread over the garden area.

- Keeping the mower in good condition to maintain the garden throughout the year.

- Getting some artificial grass for the garden to add a greener look in the not so apt seasons like winters.

Garden treatment specializes in providing winter care for the garden. They keep in mind the essentials and basics of the task by not mowing over and over again, limitlessly.

They use high-quality materials to enhance the beauty of the garden. Garden treatment also provides artificial grass solutions to their clients whenever asked. Artificial grass is a low maintenance conventional idea to add some volume to the existing lush green grass bed in the garden.

Garden service asserts the usage of the mower in the winter season as well. As mending the garden s in the cold frosty season is as important as it is in hot summers. The grass is comparatively more vulnerable in the winters thus using a leaf blower frequently might damage it.

Lightly raking the leaves seems to be a better and less harmful solution to the said problem. Garden service makes sure that your garden stays healthy in every sense in all seasons. Getting even through the winters is almost easy with the help of such professionals.

Chapter 9: Growing Herbs

Herbs have been an important part of human lives. They are used in a lot of dishes to add aroma to the meals. We often come across recipes and dishes that ask for fresh Parsley, Basil, or Chives and we end up using the dried herbs available in the market which lacks the freshness and the aroma expected of it. Now, wouldn't it be better if you could have the same herbs freshly at your home? At a cost much lower than what you pay in the market? Well, we've got a solution for this. You can now grow herbs at home at much less effort and costs. You can grow almost any kind of herb at home like Chives, parsley, Basil, Cilantro, Thyme, and much more. All these plants although require slightly different conditions to grow, however, they are not difficult to provide because it does not need much space to grow. There are a lot of benefits of growing your herbs at home, but

95

one of the major positive points is that the herbs are completely healthy and free of all kinds of additives, chemical sprays, and other genetically modified ingredients that may affect your health.

To grow herbs at home you will need to carefully set a specific portion for them at home with enough air supply. Herbs need little but regular water supply to grow in. Similarly, you will have to make sure that the herbs get enough light to get their photosynthesis properly. This way you will be able to grow natural herbs at home which would be an inexpensive, convenient and healthy choice for your regular consumption.

The Basics of Growing Herbs In Containers

Almost any herb can easily be grown in a container. However, some herbs may have different water requirements and some herbs are more particular in their watering requirements than others so it's a good idea to place herbs that have the same maintenance requirements together in the same pots.

Choosing What Herbs to Plant

Plant any herbs you like the look, taste, and smell of. Herbs such as rosemary make good candidates because depending on where you live, rosemary can be expensive to buy can be used in a wide variety of dishes, and once established, requires very little maintenance.

Soil Conditions

Most herbs require good drainage so only use high-quality potting soil and always ensure that you plant your herbs in a container that has adequate drainage holes, so you don't drown your herbs.

Choosing the Right Container for Your Herbs

Most herbs can be planted in any container as most herbs don't have larger root systems and some tolerate drying out between watering. However, keep in mind that the less soil your pot contains per plant, the less margin of error you have when it comes to watering your plants.

Multi-Plant Containers

Many smaller herbs can do well when planted next to other herbs in the same large container. If you periodically prune them, you can prevent them from competing for light. However, one plant that doesn't like being in the same pot as other herbs is basil as basil requires good air circulation.

Self-Watering Pots

Some herbs such as parsley, mint, and chives can do well in self-watering containers because they like to have a constant level of moisture. However, other herbs such as rosemary, oregano, and basil prefer dryer conditions and therefore herbs such as these should not be planted in self-watering containers.

Deciding Which Herbs to Combine In The One Container-

Generally, you can grow as many types of herbs as you like in one container provided they all have very similar soil, sun, and watering preferences. For example, parsley needs a steady supply of moisture whilst rosemary prefers dryer conditions; therefore, the two herbs should not be planted in the same pot together.

Planting Herbs in The Same Container As Different Types Of Plants

Herbs can look fantastic when planted with different types of plants such as perennials provided they have similar sun, soil, and watering requirements.

Harvesting Your Herbs

Generally, the more you pick or prune your herbs, the more they will grow. It is a good idea to regularly prune your herbs to make them more well-formed and bushier.

How to Take Care of Your Herbs

After planting your preferred fruits, vegetables, and herbs, you need to observe proper maintenance and care. Taking care of your container garden is not difficult. Still, compared to a traditional garden, a container garden needs extra watering and feeding.

Watering

Most plants need frequent watering unless otherwise stated, as in the case of Mediterranean herbs. Potting soil quickly dries out, especially during windy or hot weather. You may need to water your plants more than once a day if the weather becomes unbelievably hot. In some cases, you may need to add liquid fertilizers, and you can use your watering can for that.

To check if your plant needs more water, insert your finger into the soil. If you feel that the land within the first few inches from the top is bone dry, then you need to water your plant. Make sure that your water penetrates the roots of your plant.

Applying Fertilizer

There is a need to fertilize your plants every two weeks to make sure that they get the right amount of nutrients. Liquid fertilizer is the easiest to use because you only need to mix the fertilizer with water and pour it onto the soil down to the roots. Organic fertilizer is a wise choice.

Beware of Pests

Although a container garden is less prone to pests than a traditional garden, there is still a chance that an infestation might happen. If you notice the presence of parasites, act immediately and remove possible sources of the pests. You can also apply NEEM oil on the leaves and stems of your plants to prevent pests from invading your garden. The oil acts as a natural fungicide and pesticide. It also discourages the feeding of the pests.

Ample Sun Exposure

Plants need sunlight to thrive and grow, so make sure that your plants are getting the required amount of light. In the absence of natural light, you can use artificial lighting that still makes photosynthesis possible.

Regular Pruning

Make your plants look fresh and alive all the time by pruning them. Dead leaves can make your plant look dull and unappealing, so you need to remove the dead leaves right away. Spray the leaves with water to remove the dust.

Plants with Disease

If you suspect that a certain plant in your garden has a disease, it is best to isolate the said plant and try to cure it. If the condition becomes worse, then it is best to discard the plant as well as its soil. Using the contaminated soil of the dead plant will only cause a problem.

Some Parting Words

It may take a while before you get used to container gardening. You need to exercise patience, diligence, discipline, perseverance, and willingness to learn and discover new things. Your container garden may not look appealing now but understand that you have just begun. Your passion and your container garden need some time to bloom into something more radiant and beautiful. Be patient so that you will reap your reward.

Herbs to Grow in Your Container Garden

Basil

You'll want to grow this similar to an annual or a short-lived perennial in your container garden. Be sure to use a deep pot for this plant because it will require space for the roots. You also want well-draining soil and don't water the pot unless it's dry.

Bay

Bay is something that will grow slowly at first, but it will eventually form a small tree or a bush that you can easily train into any shape you want. You should plant bay in a large pot with soil that drains well.

Chervil

This is also known as French parsley and is an annual that is very similar in appearance and taste, with some undertones of anise. To harvest this plant, snip the outer leaves and the stems. Be sure that this is in soil that drains well and water it regularly.

Chives

These plants look a lot like grass and are perennial that have a slight onion flavor. They're a prolific producer in container gardens and have a mild taste. Cut off small bunches back to the soil level and allow the rest to grow. Chives like soil that is slightly damp but be sure there is still adequate drainage. They're an excellent choice of plants for beginners.

Cilantro

Cilantro is also known as Chinese parsley and is a short-lived annual that has a citrusy, parsley flavor. It is better when you start it from the seed as it grows out quickly, but when it's harvested, it doesn't grow back. Extend the harvest by growing a few pots in different stages. Cilantro also likes soil that drains well and well-aerated.

Dill

It's better when you grow dill indoors for the leaves because it will be hard to get it to seed and get a nice harvest. Sow a few pots at different intervals for a nice supply. Fernleaf is an excellent, compact variety that enjoys being grown in a container.

Marjoram

Marjoram comes from the Mediterranean area and is in the oregano family, but the flavor is a lot sweeter and more delicate. It's often grown in containers indoors.

Mints

Spearmint and Peppermint are great choices for container gardens when they are the only plant in the pot. They can easily take over the entire pot and should be planted alone. Be sure to keep the soil on the drier side.

Parsley

Curly leaf and flat-leaf parsley are excellent choices for growing inside containers both indoors and outdoors. The Italian variety is biennial and has a very robust flavor. When you harvest from the plant, cut the outer leaves. This encourages new growth at the center and keeps the parsley alive and productive.

Rosemary

Rosemary comes in two different forms, trailing and upright. The blue boy variety is compact and has a robust flavor, as well as the Salem or Taylor's blue. Even though this herb likes dry conditions, you shouldn't let the soil dry out completely since it will die.

Sage

You'll want to grow the twelve-inch dwarf sage for container gardening or a nonflowering variety like berggarten. Dwarf sage has the same flavor as a garden sage but only gets ten to twelve inches high. Keep sage in a well-draining potting mix and fertilize it when needed.

Thyme

There are many different varieties of thyme, but the best ones for container gardening are the French thyme and the Lemon thyme. You can also try the oregano thyme, which is a trailing variety.

Ornamental

Most herbs can also be used ornamentally if you'd like, but some have very beautiful flowers, an enticing aroma, and a deep green or unique foliage that adds a bit of flair to a container herb garden. Look at some of these ornamental herbs you could use to spice things up!

Silver Thyme

Silver thyme will get about twelve inches tall and has lavender to pink blossom in the summer months. It's an evergreen that will need a twelve-inch-wide by twelve-inch-deep pot to flourish. The fragrant, silver leaves make a bushy texture in the garden. It loves sunny locations and prefers sandier soil. It's also an excellent addition to tea and sauces if you feel inclined to harvest it.

Oregano Blooms

Origanum leavigatum has a purple to pink blossom that blooms for a long time. It grows to about two feet tall and has dark green leaves with a purple tint. Unfortunately, these herbs are not very good for cooking, but they do have a beautiful scent and a nice appearance. Herrenhausen has masses of pink flowers that have maroon bracts on the purple stems while Hopleys is a taller plant with long-blooming, deep pink stems.

Oregano can easily grow to about a foot high in pots and has a spicy flavor. When you harvest the leaves, you encourage the plant to grow even more, and the plant will remain productive for up to two years. When the plant becomes woody, it should be replaced.

Roman Chamomile

Chamaemelum nobile is a one-foot-tall plant with white blossoms that bloom all summer long. It's extremely aromatic with an apple to pineapple scent. The threadlike leaves can also be used in teas; the young leaves are the ones you want to use for your tea. In the summer, the blossoms are white with an almost daisy-like appearance. This herb loves moist, rich soil and will grow to a foot tall in a proper pot.

Berggarten Sage

Also known as Salvia, this two-foot-tall plant blooms in the early summer and has violet to blue flowers. The foliage is compact, shapely leaves that are dark green. At two feet tall, it's perfect as a backdrop for shorter container plants in the front. The dusty green leaves are a beautiful background for almost any container garden. You can also use the leaves medicinally as a tea to treat throat and lung problems. This sage can also be used to flavor meats and potatoes.

Catmint

Nepeta X Faassenii is an herb that cats adore and is also known as catnip in many regions of the globe. It's an eighteen-inch tall, bushy plant when it's in the right conditions, and has lavender blossoms that will bloom all through the summer. It also attracts many beneficial insects to the garden with its blooms, so while it's not normally edible for people, it can be used in container gardens to attract bees and other small insects to pollinate vegetables.

Catmint light green foliage and should be cut back throughout the season to encourage it to bush out and blossom more.

Salem Rosemary

Rosmarinus officinalis or 'Salem' makes a beautiful, two-foot-long backdrop for many other plants that bloom. The blossoms on this herb are a nice blue color and it's an early bloomer in the spring, so it provides color where many herbs are not yet able to bloom. It's an evergreen that has green, shiny needle leaves that weave through the container like thread. You can prune it down to the level you'd like throughout the growing season and use the pieces you harvest in soups and stews after you've dried them.

This plant likes fertile soil, a lot of drainages, and plenty of sunlight.

Cardoon

Cardoon has a purple blossom that makes itself known in the mid-summer and grows to around five feet tall. Therefore, it's best planted on its own in a large pot to keep it happy. It has gray-green leaves that arch and frame to showcase the purple thistle-like flowers. This herb is also edible. The stalks and leaves can be blanched and consumed, as well as the unopened flower heads.

This plant prefers a sunny, well-drained area.

Sweet Cicely

Myrrhis odorata is a late spring bloomer with white flowers that grow around two to four feet tall. This is a shade-tolerant herb that has a fernlike appearance that grows in a mound with bright-green leaves. In the late spring, it's topped with a white star-shaped flower that has a shiny brown seed when it's finished. It does the best in partial to full shade in moist, rich soil.

The seeds and leaves have a sweet anise flavor that goes well with desserts, especially those made with fruits.

Anise Hyssop

This plant has a bright red bloom that appears in the late summer. The plant grows to about two to six feet tall, depending on the container it's placed in, and has gray-green leaves. This plant prefers a well-drained, sunny area.

The flowers have an appealing taste, like sweet anise, and it's delicious in salads. This is also another plant that's excellent for attracting bees and other beneficial insects to the garden.

Garlic Chives

Allium tuberosum has a white bloom that appears in the late summer. The plant grows to eighteen inches tall and prefers a sunny location with sandy, fertile soil. It also blends in well with its neighbors, like a flowering tobacco plant or some coneflowers. It has starry white flowers that catch the eye easily. After the flowers bloom, it's best to cut any of the seeds' heads off and use them for decorative purposes because the seeds are vigorous growers. The flat, garlic-flavored leaves can be picked throughout the growing season to add to sauces, soups, and dips.

Frequently Asked Questions About Herb Gardening

Which Herbs Can I Begin With?

The truth is, hundreds of herbs are available in repositories, and you can cultivate them for their medicinal and culinary benefits. However, the most important factors that you have to consider when choosing the right herbs will be what you want to grow, and other essential conditions that support your herbs of choice such as the soil and the climate.

The best thing is for you to assess a list of herbs that you have in mind and determine which ones you are your favorite and fit into the growth conditions available in your location.

What Cultural Requirements Do the Herbs Have?

For each herb to thrive well, you must know the required conditions for its optimal growth. Other plants also can self-propagate, in which case you are fortunate if one of your herbs does this. Self-propagation refers to the ability of a plant to self-reproduce either by reseeding, layering, cutting, among other ways.

The most important thing is to pay close attention to the amount of sun the herbs need each day. The information that you can get from journals, and if it says that they need it for 4-6 hours in a day, then it probably needs just that! The other thing is water requirements and the soil type it needs. It ensures that they get optimal conditions for optimal growth and development.

Which Herbs Can I Plant Considering My Weather?

When it comes to the choice of herbs to plant in your climate, you can replicate each herb's requirements. For instance, most of the herbs do well with less water, 4-6 hours of sunlight exposure, and average quality soil.

However, when it comes to winter temperatures, the conditions cannot be compromised. It means that you must be within the zone that your herbs of choice can thrive. You can also find this information available at the nursery where these herb seedlings are raised.

The truth is, determining the kinds of herbs that will do well within your area. You will realize that if you come from a place where the conditions are delicate; you can grow a few of those that need this kind of terms specifically. You can also substitute those you cannot grow in your area.

Should I Raise My Herbs from Seeds?

Seeds are the best when it comes to herb gardening, especially if you are a beginner. Remember that we have mentioned getting seeds from reputable companies that have not genetically engineered their components. In fact, rather than getting your seeds just from one company, you can get them from at least two companies.

It is also crucial that you ensure that you have read the herb's descriptions well.

The best thing is to consider a suitable vendor to work with. To do that, consider asking yourself the following questions:

- Which company meets the criteria you are looking for?

- Will the company be a suitable resource for educational materials?

- Is their process of ordering helpful?

- What is their client service?

- Do they have ethical considerations when it comes to GMOs, hybrid seeds, and SEMINIS?

- Don't worry if you feel like you are not ready yet to raise herbs from seeds. The truth is that you will finally get where you are going, and the best thing is for you to start with the goal in mind.

Where Can I Find Herb Plants?

If you desire to start a medicinal or culinary herb garden, there is a good chance that you will exhaust so many resources available in local nurseries within a couple of years. It is because, by the time you have mastered all that information, you will already be herb-savvy! It is because you will have moved from pure herbs like basil to a broader and more intricate variety.

However, if you are specifically looking for culinary and medicinal herbs, the best place you can get them is from Horizon Herbs. The best thing about this place is that they offer you satisfactory answers to your questions that revolve around; what seeds are viable. They also have packets, catalogs, and experts who are knowledgeable about herbs. They sell container herbs and cuttings from the roots, which can be very helpful, especially if you do not wish to start from growing seeds.

Can I Grow Herbs from Seeds?

If you have a friend, family, or local nursery growing herbs, you can gather information from them on the best methods of rooting or cutting for that herb and then try to replicate it.

For instance, what I have found out about thyme over the years is that they can be propagated so well and easily by layering. It is how you can achieve successful layering by first taking a supple thyme stem that is mature and sits it in the soil. Use a garden pin to weigh that down. Ensure that you have it watered well and then wait for it to begin sprouting at the soil surface. Then cut it off to get new herbs. Hence no seed is required.

Again, you must ensure that you have reference material on hand. It is also vital for you to learn how to perform wild crafts, especially for those plants that you have available and where it is legal.

Chapter 10: Growing and Harvesting

Can't choose between sowing or buying seedlings ready for transplantation? It depends on the time you have available and the willingness to experiment with a chance, that of sowing, which requires a bit of trust and patience and the respect of a few simple rules.

Seeding

The use of sowing offers many advantages, not least that of being able to choose from a wider range of species and varieties.

Many vegetables (cut salads, spinach, radishes, carrots, peas, beans) cannot stand transplanting, so they must be sown directly in the ground. Using seeds will also allow you to obtain some varieties of vegetables specially selected for the pots and usually not available among the ready-to-transplant species for sale in Garden Centers. And then, witnessing the birth of a seedling is always an exciting spectacle that is part of the pleasures of gardening. It is not worth, on the contrary, to sow the species with a very long germination time, because they would oblige you to prolong for weeks the assiduous care to be reserved to the seedbeds.

When Is It Better in Seedbeds?

For some vegetables, sowing in seedbeds is more suitable, while those that cannot stand transplanting must be buried directly in the pot in which they will be harvested: the seed sachets always indicate where sowing is to take place.

The protected environment of a seedbed, which, if necessary, can also be transported indoors, makes it possible to anticipate sowing times, as well as offering more favorable heat and humidity conditions for germination.

Any container, if it is perforated at the bottom and about 4 inches deep, can serve as a seedbed.

Low fruit crates with plastic trays are also suitable, or egg containers (both of which must be drilled). These containers can then be covered with a transparent plastic sheet to reduce temperature changes and keep the environment moist; thus, favoring the rapid germination of the seeds,

If you want to use the many models of seedbeds on the market, you will be spoilt for choice: plastic trays with transparent lid and cell inserts (very practical: to take the seedlings once they are ready for transplanting just press the bottom of the cell and push them upwards), or long and narrow containers designed for windowsills, and also seedbeds equipped with electrical resistances that allow maintaining a constant temperature.

Larger seeds (such as Cucumbers and Courgettes/Zucchini) can also be buried in jars where they will remain until transplanting in their final container, while vegetables with delicate roots can be avoided the shock of transplanting by seeding them in peat pots to be planted in the last location after the seedling is born.

Tricks of the Trade - How To Store Seeds

Probably the sachets on the market, however small, will always be oversized concerning your needs. You can then exchange the advanced seeds with some friends who are fond of vegetable gardens or keep them for the following year. In this case, they must be protected from humidity and light so that they do not lose their germination capacity.

Fold the edge of the sachet twice and seal it with a clip. Or transfer the seeds into an airtight container, such as the tubes of effervescent tablets: the absorbent pad fixed on the cap will ensure that your seeds are free of moisture. Then place the sachets or tubes in a dry place.

Good Rules

Some rules apply to obtain good results both in the case of seedbed sowing and directly in the pot.

Sowing must be done at the right depth (which is equal to the largest diameter of the seed) and at the right time (this is indicated on the seed sachets).

The seedbeds should be filled with seeding soil up to about 3/8 inches from the edge. Then press the soil lightly and use a toothpick to drill a hole of the stable depth in which the seed is placed or draw grooves and deposit the seeds at a distance indicated on the package.

Cover the seeds with soil, possibly mixed with sand, and wet by spraying water with a vaporizer adjusted to the minimum so that the seeds do not sink into the ground. To keep the temperature constant, cover the seedbed with a transparent cover or plastic sheet. The soil must be kept moist, but not soaked, and the seedbed must be checked at least once a day to ensure that the soil does not dry out too much. In order not to make any confusion, accompany the seedbeds with tags indicating the different species.

When the first sprouts appear (germination times vary from one vegetable to another, see table), you can start to remove the lid during the hottest hours to avoid the formation of mold. Then it will be eliminated, and the watering will be spaced a bit apart, and, in the case of too thick sowing, the seedlings will thin out, eliminating the weaker ones.

For sowing directly at the planting site, proceed in the same way except for the soil of the pots, which will not be a sowing soil but the one intended to feed the plant throughout the season. Often out of impatience, people tend to anticipate the sowing. Still, if the light is poor and the temperature is too low, the seeds germinate and develop very slowly, and this makes them more susceptible to diseases and attacks of parasites. So for outdoor sowing, it is better to wait until the end of February - the beginning of March. And finally, one last piece of advice: both cats and birds are irresistibly attracted to the loose soil; to avoid irreparable damage to the freshly sown pots, you can cover them with a wide-meshed net until the seedlings have grown.

The Germination Times

They are indicative because they can vary depending on the temperature (the higher it is, the faster the germination), the type of soil, and its degree of humidity. They also depend on the condition of the seeds, those stored correctly germinate faster.

The Transplant

To strengthen their root system, when the seedlings born in seedbeds have emitted the first two real small leaves, they are to be transferred in single jars, which, however, are not yet the definitive ones. This is done by gently extracting the seedling from the soil with a flat stick and placing it in the new pot filled with garden earth lightened with a little sand. Place the pots in a corner sheltered from the sun and drafts and then water them gently, keeping the soil slightly moist for a few days to prevent the roots from drying out.

After some time, when the seedlings are well strengthened and have issued the first 4-8 leaves, you can proceed with the final transplanting.

First, prepare the pot that will house the plant for the whole season: place a piece of broken pot on the drainage hole, arranging it in such a way that it does not hermetically close the hole but only prevents the soil from blocking it. Then, to ensure good drainage, distribute on the bottom a layer of expanded clay (or gravel) about 1/6 of the height of the container. At this point, begin to fill the pot with the potting soil by pressing it lightly with your hands: never reach the edge of the pot, but always leave a border of an inch to allow adequate irrigation. Dig a hole wide enough to accommodate the seedling.

Take out from the pot the seedling with the bread of earth, trying not to break it, and bury it in the new pot, checking that the collar, that is the part of the stem in contact with the roots, is at ground level (plants buried too deeply risk rotting). Squeeze the soil a little more and water it moderately to further compact the soil and to offer a providential water supply to the newcomer. Repeat the watering every evening until the young plants have settled in. At this stage, the pot should stay out of direct sunlight. If you are afraid of a return of cold, you should also think about protecting the most delicate species during the night. You can use a transparent plastic bottle, for example, a mineral water bottle: cut it in half and put the part with the neck in the ground, but without the cap.

When the plant will be strengthened, the bottle will be removed. Or you can use the protective bells on sale in specialist shops.

The seedlings purchased ready for transplanting should be transplanted following the same procedure as those sown on their own. Always check their state of health at the time of purchase. The best ones have a strong stem and a compact appearance. Avoid those with diseased, soft, or withered leaves, and those with roots coming out from the bottom of the pot: their stay in the pot has been too long.

Harvesting

Also, for the harvest, one of the most pleasant moments that your hobby has in store for you, it will be useful for you some tricks if you want good-looking and well-preserved vegetables. These are simple rules of common sense, but it is good to remember them:

Vegetables from bulb and root: in order not to damage Garlic, Shallot, Carrot, Red Beet, and Radish at harvest time, grab them and lift them only after gently moving the soil with a hoe.

Leafy vegetables: those that do not regrow: such as Lettuce, Endive, Escarole, Radicchio, Spinach, Celery, should be picked when they are well developed and tender (in any case before they go to seed), uprooting them.

If they were in the open air instead of in a pot, you could cut them at the base leaving the roots in the ground. Salads such as Chicory, Chards, Cutting Lettuce, should be cut with the knife just above the collar after each regrowth when they are tender.

121

Fruit vegetables: Melons are detached with the hands, using the circular groove that forms around the stalk. Cucumbers are best removed with scissors, when they begin to lose their spines, while Courgettes are best removed by hand with a twisting movement or by cutting the stalk when they are still tender or even with the flower still attached. Tomatoes are picked by hand or, in cluster varieties, with scissors. Peppers should not be picked before they start to color; it's best to use scissors because the stalk is hard, and the branches are fragile. Peas, Beans, and Green Beans must be removed with the hands very gently so as not to break the tender climbing branches.

Aromatic Herbs: the Parsley should be cut with the knife a couple of centimeters above the collar, even cutting it in an integral way the Parsley regrows anyway. Basil should be trimmed vigorously: the plant will come back from the bottom, remaining beautifully leafy and becoming stronger. Sage, Rosemary, Thyme, and other Aromatics: cut the outer twigs with scissors if you want to keep the foliage compact and in shape; otherwise, trim them vigorously.

Conclusion

Once you begin container gardening, you will be hooked on the concept for good. You will not only be able to brag to your friends and family about what you have accomplished, but you will have peace of mind in knowing exactly where your food came from and what it was subjected to. How many of your friends and family members can say that with assurance?

Growing fruit and vegetables in a pot do take a little planning and consideration. However, it is certainly worth taking the time to consider all the factors which will affect your fruit production. By ensuring that you have created a hospitable environment for your fruiting plants to flourish, you could create a healthy and happy plant, which will produce fruit for many years to come. This small investment in time and energy could allow you and your family to enjoy fresh home-grown fruit throughout the year. The extended growing season resulting from the stable temperatures within your home could allow you to produce a higher yield of fantastic quality fruits the whole family will enjoy.

This book has taught you everything you need to know to get started with your private container garden. Although the concept can seem daunting at first, you will be amazed at how much you get into the process and how much fun you can have with it.

123

Chances are you will end up growing more food than you can consume. This means sharing it with others or, if you prefer, selling it on the side. Either way, it's a good feeling to know that the rewards of your hard work can be shared and enjoyed by others.

Being able to count on a crop of your favorite fruits and vegetables year after year is rewarding in and of itself. But knowing that you not only had a hand in their availability, from concept to harvesting, and that you did it all by yourself does make the food taste that much better.

Happy container gardening!

CPSIA information can be obtained
at www.ICGtesting.com
Printed in the USA
BVHW081012070421
604341BV00006B/752